MW00634656

The White House Easter Egg Roll

A History for All Ages

The White House Easter Egg Roll
A History for All Ages

by Jonathan Pliska

illustrations by John Hutton

THE WHITE HOUSE *HISTORICAL ASSOCIATION*

THE WHITE HOUSE HISTORICAL ASSOCIATION is a nonprofit educational association founded in 1961 for the purpose of enhancing the understanding, appreciation, and enjoyment of the Executive Mansion. All proceeds from the sale of the Association's books and products are used to fund the acquisition of historic furnishings and art work for the permanent White House collection, assist in the preservation of public rooms, and further its educational mission.

BOARD OF DIRECTORS
Frederick J. Ryan Jr., Chairman
John F. W. Rogers, Vice Chairman
James I. McDaniel, Secretary
John T. Behrendt, Treasurer
Stewart D. McLaurin, President

Jean Case, Henry A. Dudley Jr., Cathy Gorn, Janet A. Howard, Knight Kiplinger, Martha Joynt Kumar, Anita McBride, Mike McCurry, Robert M. McGee, Roger B. Porter, Ann S. Stock, Ben C. Sutton Jr., Tina Tchen

Ex Officio: David Ferriero, Carla Hayden, Tom Mayes, Earl A. Powell III, David Skorton

Emeritis: Nash Castro, Jeannine S. Clark, John H. Dalton, Nancy M. Folger, Elise K. Kirk, Harry G. Robinson III, Leonard L. Silverstein, Gail Berry West

Vice President of Publishing and Executive Editor: Marcia Mallet Anderson
Editorial Director: Fiona Griffin • Senior Production Manager: Lauren Zook McGwin
Production Manager: Kristin Skinner • Editorial Assistant: Jeanine Marie
Consulting Editor: Ann Hofstra Grogg • Designer: Bruce Kenselaar

Copyright © 2018 White House Historical Association.
All rights reserved under international copyright conventions. No part of this book may be reproduced or utilized in any form or by any means, electronic or mechanical, including photocopying, recording, or by any information storage and retrieval system, without permission in writing from the publisher.

First Edition
10 9 8 7 6 5 4 3 2 1
Library of Congress Control Number: 2017958800
ISBN 978-1-931917-86-5
Printed in the United States of America

Following a tradition that began in 1878, the president and first lady welcome children and their families onto the White House Grounds to celebrate Easter Monday with a fun-filled day that is now one of the oldest, and most popular, annual events in the history of the White House. The lucky guests gather to roll brightly dyed hard-boiled eggs down the sloped South Lawn, and over the years other activities—games, music, story-time, and dancing to name only a few—have been added to ensure that everyone has a good time.

The White House Grounds, which span more than 18 acres of parkland, are perfect for rolling Easter Eggs, but the South Lawn has always been the president's backyard, a place where the first family relaxes. The yearly Easter Egg Roll is a special opportunity for the public to come inside the fence and enjoy this beautiful space too.

Children take great delight in rolling their eggs—and themselves!— down a pair of small hills that have stood on either side of the White House as far back as anyone can remember. For many years experts thought that our third president, Thomas Jefferson, built these hills in the early 1800s, but now archaeologists and historians think the so-called "Jefferson Mounds" were actually created in the 1820s by President James Monroe.

Sprays of water from the grand South Fountain would be a great way for egg-rollers to cool off when the hot, humid D.C. summers come early but no wading is allowed! President Ulysses S. Grant installed the fountain in 1876, two years before the tradition of the White House Easter Egg Roll began.

Two elegant gardens provide a backdrop of flowers and ornamental plants for the annual egg roll. President John F. Kennedy's famous Rose Garden was planted on the west side of the White House in 1962, and the garden on the east side was named for his wife, First Lady Jacqueline Kennedy, in 1965.

Great groves of trees offer wonderful play spaces for children and welcome shade for parents. There are hundreds of trees that dot the landscape, and at least one might be even older than the White House itself. Many others were personally planted by the presidents and first ladies. The oldest of these commemorative trees is a Japanese maple planted by First Lady Frances Cleveland in 1893. President John Quincy Adams planted an American elm near the base of the eastern "Jefferson Mound" in 1826. When this historic tree died in 1991, First Lady Barbara Bush replaced it with a new elm grafted from the original tree.

Presidents Andrew Johnson and Ulysses S. Grant are said to have hosted the first White House Egg Rolls in the 1860s and 1870s, but they were small gatherings limited to family and close friends. First Lady Eliza Johnson, who was a frail woman, sat on the South Portico and delighted in watching her grandchildren play. The three youngest Grant children—Buck, Nellie, and Jesse—always attracted attention when they set foot on the grounds, and they are likely the first presidential kids to roll eggs at Easter.

But the biggest and best egg rolls from this time took place down the street, on the grounds of the United States Capitol. Just when this custom began is uncertain, but Capitol Hill had been hosting crowds of happy children for many decades. One story holds that First Lady Dolley Madison first suggested a public egg roll in 1814.

The children always enjoyed themselves very much on Capitol Hill, but they also left a terrible mess behind every year. Tired of cleaning up after them, Congress finally outlawed egg-rolling on the Capitol Grounds after the 1876 event. Although the news came as a sad shock to the children, a bad rainstorm kept everyone indoors in 1877.

President Rutherford B. Hayes came to the rescue in 1878, when he invited the youngsters to come and roll their eggs at the White House. About two hundred children quickly accepted his offer and made themselves quite at home on the South Lawn. The annual White House Easter Egg Roll had officially begun!

President James Garfield kept the gates open after Hayes left office, and made sure that the egg-rolling holiday continued. The next president, Chester A. Arthur, really got into the spirit of things by going out into the crowd to introduce himself to the adults and play with the children. His own 10-year-old daughter, Ellen, made many new friends and quickly became the life of the party.

President Grover Cleveland celebrated his first White House Easter Egg Roll in 1885. At the end of the day, he invited the children into the grand East Room to shake their hands. The delighted kiddies rushed inside, grinding bits of smashed egg and broken eggshells into the plush carpet as they went. But the jolly president either didn't notice or didn't care, and he continued to hold these indoor receptions every year.

In 1889, President Benjamin Harrison thrilled the crowd by adding live music to the Easter Egg Roll. With his two-year-old grandson, he stepped onto the South Portico just as the U.S. Marine Band, known as "The President's Own," struck up a rousing march. Led by famed conductor John Philip Sousa, the band performed all day for the children's entertainment. These concerts quickly became a highlight of the annual White House Easter Egg Roll, and the Marine Band continues to provide entertaining music to this day.

President Cleveland returned to the White House for a second term in 1893, and enthusiastically resumed his role as host for the Easter Monday festivities. His young daughters, Ruth and Esther, eagerly joined the fun, as did their mother, First Lady Frances Cleveland, who "romped and played" like a schoolgirl. Cleveland himself happily tried his luck at "egg picking," a game in which rivals took turns knocking hard-boiled eggs together; scoring a win if the opponent's egg cracked first. Children organized other games too—"egg ball," "toss and catch," and even "egg croquet." Before long, the odor of broken eggs could be smelled 3 miles away.

The first Easter Egg Roll of the twentieth century took place on April 8, 1901, during the presidency of William McKinley. By now, kids and adults alike looked forward to the occasion all year long, and as many as 50,000 people attended in a single year. Despite this immense surge in popularity, the setting itself had changed very little since Hayes's tenure. The White House Grounds appeared frozen in time, but change was just around the corner.

One year later, in 1902 President Theodore Roosevelt expanded the White House by building the West Wing, which holds the Oval Office. In order to clear space for this extension, he demolished a vast complex of greenhouses that had supplied the mansion with flowers since before the Civil War.

But all was not lost, as First Lady Edith Roosevelt
designed two new gardens, the ancestors of the Rose
Garden and the Jacqueline Kennedy Garden, that
bloomed with snapdragons, goldenrods, and other
old-fashioned favorites. For the first time, current
visitors to the White House Easter Egg Roll would
have recognized the South Lawn as it exists today.

With the popular Roosevelts in the White House, attendance at the Easter Egg Roll grew so huge that something had to be done. In 1905, adults were banned unless accompanied by a child. But those denied entry simply resorted to "borrowing" children from outside the gates, and opportunistic kids quickly realized they could earn some pocket money from the change in policy.

At least one boy made a small fortune, a dime at a time, by escorting wave after wave of new "parents" onto the South Lawn.

William Howard Taft, the only person to serve as both president of the United States and chief justice of the Supreme Court, continued to welcome children onto the White House Grounds for the annual Easter Egg Roll. President Woodrow Wilson cheerfully followed the tradition until 1917, when America's entry into World War I forced an unprecedented change. Because of safety concerns, the event was moved to the Washington Monument Grounds, marking the first time in forty years that the public was not allowed to roll eggs on the South Lawn.

In 1918, in order to save some 60 million eggs for the war effort, the nation observed an "eggless Easter," and the White House Easter Egg Roll was officially cancelled for the first time in its history. The only visitors to the grounds that year were a flock of eighteen sheep, who grazed on the grass and helped conserve both gasoline and manpower. The government auctioned off the sheep's wool, earning the American Red Cross $52,823. Continued food rationing also stopped the egg roll in 1919 and 1920.

President Warren G. Harding and his wife, First Lady Florence Harding, took great pleasure in resuming the annual White House Easter Egg Roll in 1921. After a three-year interruption, the holiday once again drew capacity crowds, even when the presidential couple were not personally in attendance. Such was the case in 1923, when the Hardings' pet dog, an Airedale terrier named Laddie Boy, "hosted" the day in their stead.

1921~The White House EGG Roll Returns!

On April 18, 1927, First Lady Grace Coolidge, wife of President Calvin Coolidge, introduced her egg-rolling guests to Rebecca, her pet raccoon. Rebecca had been sent to the Coolidges as a gift from Mississippi to be part of the White House Thanksgiving feast the previous fall. But she was surprisingly friendly and well-behaved, and so wound up as one of the most unusual presidential pets of all time. When not presiding over Easter Egg Rolls, Rebecca lived in her own tree house, bathed in the White House bathtubs, draped herself around the president's neck, and fell asleep in Mrs. Coolidge's arms.

In 1929, the White House Easter Egg Roll took place on April Fools' Day, but there were no pranks or tricks. Concerned that there might not be enough eggs to go around, President Herbert Hoover had a crate of eggs that had been given to him by the governor of Kansas hard-boiled, dyed in bright colors, and handed out to the children. First Lady Lou Hoover put her own stamp on the day by inviting Girl Scouts to perform traditional Native American, Swedish, and English folk dances around a maypole. The White House Easter Egg Roll was also broadcast live on the radio for the first time; the Marine Band's music was heard but neither the president nor first lady spoke.

From 1933 to 1941, Franklin Delano Roosevelt presided over nine White House Easter Egg Rolls, more than any other president. During the 1933 event, First Lady Eleanor Roosevelt greeted visitors and listeners for the first time over the radio, on a nationwide hookup. In 1937 the Easter Egg Roll set an attendance record of 53,180. Three years later, on a bitterly cold Easter Monday, a mere 5,480 children and adults passed through the White House gates before noon. Speaking to the small but dedicated group, Mrs. Roosevelt hoped that they would all "run around, play, and keep warm."

Following U.S. entry into World War II in December 1941, the Easter Egg Roll was moved from the White House Grounds to the Capitol Grounds. So in 1942 Easter Eggs and children rolled down Capitol Hill for the first time in sixty-four years. 132,000 children and adults enjoyed the day. But it was not to last. Wartime security measures completely shut down the festivities from 1943 to 1945.

A victim of bad luck and poor timing, Harry S. Truman was the only president in the twentieth century to have never held an Easter Egg Roll. Food conservation efforts caused him to reluctantly cancel the occasion in 1946 and 1947. By this time the White House was nearly 150 years old and in desperate need of a complete renovation. To save the historic mansion, the president had it torn down to its bare walls and rebuilt. From 1948 to 1952 the South Lawn was one big construction site, making it impossible to stage the annual egg roll.

under
Construction
NO
egg roll
this year

The Egg Roll Returns!

After a twelve-year lapse, President Dwight D. Eisenhower revived the customary White House Easter Egg Roll on April 6, 1953. First Lady Mamie Eisenhower, who loved all kinds of parties, helped with the planning. During her husband's eight years in office, she cheerfully served as hostess at countless receptions, dinners, and ceremonies. The Eisenhowers' final Easter Egg Roll, held on April 18, 1960, also marked the last presidential appearance at the event for sixteen years. The next three presidents—John F. Kennedy, Lyndon B. Johnson, and Richard Nixon—were all not able to attend in person.

JFK LBJ RN

The National Park Service took over responsibility for the care and maintenance of the White House Grounds during President Kennedy's term. A playground installed on the South Lawn for the Kennedys' four-year-old daughter, Caroline, attracted a great deal of attention from children at the 1962 egg roll, and White House guards had to patiently explain that Caroline wouldn't be able to play with them since she was away at the time with her parents in Palm Beach, Florida.

from L.B.J.

Sharp-eyed visitors to the White House Easter Egg Roll during the Kennedy years would have also spotted another new addition to the grounds: a pony shed that housed the family's two ponies, Macaroni and Tex, gifts from Vice President Lyndon Johnson. By the time Johnson became president himself in 1963, costumed performers dressed as the Easter Bunny were added to entertain the crowds.

In April 1969, a member of First Lady Pat Nixon's staff put on a white jumpsuit and Peter Rabbit mask and greeted children along the South Lawn's circular driveway. Mrs. Nixon's staff also arranged the first—and last—egg hunt with actual eggs. After a few days the smell of unfound eggs made them rethink the idea. On April 15, 1974, volunteers dressed as clowns organized the first egg roll races, borrowing spoons from the White House kitchen. The winning children each earned a "Nixon" ballpoint pen, and all egg-rollers received certificates of participation. Since then, these races have become an Easter Monday favorite.

In 1976, President Gerald Ford and First Lady Betty Ford became the first presidential couple to attend the Easter Egg Roll since the Eisenhowers in 1960. Mrs. Ford introduced Ukrainian egg-decorating demonstrations and gave out plastic eggs with a printed note inside as souvenirs. Plastic eggs were also used in the egg roll that year, but real eggs returned in 1977.

President Jimmy Carter and First Lady Rosalynn Carter welcomed guests to their first White House Easter Egg Roll in 1977. The president hoisted his grandson, Jason, onto his shoulders and shook hands with the crowd, while Mrs. Carter distributed 10,000 souvenir plastic eggs with a welcome message inside. The Carters also set up a petting zoo for the children to enjoy. This small circus featured dozens of animals, including bunnies, of course, but also a humongous 1,200-pound steer.

In 1981, President Ronald Reagan and First Lady Nancy Reagan brought in entertainers dressed as superheroes and cartoon characters and they added Broadway shows and giant balloons to the day's list of amusements. Mrs. Reagan, who had attended the White House Easter Egg Roll as a little girl, also introduced a hunt for wooden eggs that bore the signatures of famous people. Children searched straw pits for these autographed prizes, and wooden eggs soon became the official White House Easter Egg Roll keepsakes. The eggs are now designed to reflect the unique theme of each year's event, and feature the signatures of the president and first lady.

On March 27, 1989, President George H. W. Bush and First Lady Barbara Bush, with several of their children and grandchildren and "First Dog" Millie, an English springer spaniel, hosted their first White House Easter Egg Roll. The kitchen staff hard-boiled and colored 5,000 real eggs for the egg roll races, but wooden eggs—23,000 of them—were used for egg hunts. Vice President Dan Quayle and wife Marilyn filled in for the president and first lady in 1991, but Mrs. Bush provided heartfelt Easter cards to be mailed to the troops in the Persian Gulf. That year, all the wooden eggs were painted yellow to honor the soldiers serving in Iraq and Kuwait during Operation Desert Storm.

For their first Easter Monday celebration in 1993, President Bill Clinton and First Lady Hillary Clinton expanded the White House Easter Egg Roll to include the grounds of the Ellipse below the South Lawn, but otherwise scaled back the day's fanfare. The Clintons chose to focus on time-honored egg-rolling games that have long defined the event. The next year, their cat Socks good-naturedly lent his paw print to the design of the commemorative wooden egg. In 1998, the White House Easter Egg Roll was streamed live over the internet for the first time, allowing people everywhere to remotely share in the fun.

President George W. Bush and First Lady Laura Bush celebrated the first White House Easter Egg Roll of the twenty-first century in 2001. Two years later, in 2003, they closed the general egg roll and replaced it with a smaller event for children of active duty and reserve military personnel serving in Iraq and Afghanistan. About 12,000 people attended. The White House Easter Egg Roll reopened to the public in 2004.

President Barack Obama and First Lady Michelle Obama hosted the White House Easter Egg Roll for eight years, from 2009 through 2016. They used the event to stress the importance of a healthy, active lifestyle. As part of her "Let's Move!" campaign, Mrs. Obama used fresh fruits and vegetables harvested from the White House Kitchen Garden to create a "kid's kitchen," where chefs showed children how to make tasty, nutritious snacks. She also staged an obstacle course to promote daily exercise, and the president shot hoops with children on the White House Basketball Court. Since 2009, tickets to the White House Easter Egg Roll have been distributed via an online lottery, allowing people from across the United States an equal chance to attend in person.

President Donald Trump and First Lady Melania Trump first welcomed children to the South Lawn in 2017 to participate in the annual White House Easter Egg Roll. The president and first lady, together with their son, Barron, kicked things off at 7:30 a.m., and the festivities continued until 7:00 p.m. President and Mrs. Trump each blew a whistle to signal the start of their first egg roll race, with the president's own grandchildren enthusiastically taking part in the historic moment. Later on, the first lady read aloud from children's books while seated in a specially-built reading nook just outside the Oval Office. She was joined throughout the day by many of President Trump's cabinet members and advisers.

WHITE HOUSE TREES

The first trees and shrubs planted on the White House Grounds arrived by mail in March 1809, the same month that James Madison became the fourth president of the United States. The two most famous trees on the grounds—a pair of grand, old southern magnolias—are located immediately west of the South Portico. Although long said to have been planted by President Andrew Jackson in about 1830 as a tribute to his late wife, Rachel, little is certain about the origin of the Jackson magnolias, which remain iconic sentinels on the landscape to this day.

It was President Rutherford B. Hayes, the originator of the White House Easter Egg Roll, who popularized the custom of commemorative tree planting at the White House. Since the 1870s, many presidents and first ladies have planted commemorative trees, but sadly not all of these trees have survived. It is important to realize that because trees are living things, change is inevitable—even at the White House.

THE NORTH GROUNDS

The north front of the White House faces 1600 Pennsylvania Avenue, overlooking Lafayette Park in Washington, D.C. The North Grounds are more or less the president's front yard, with a liberal scattering of shade trees, lush grass, a fountain, and driveway. Among the special trees in the landscape are a white oak planted by President Franklin D. Roosevelt and a yulan magnolia planted by First Lady Nancy Reagan.

THE SOUTH GROUNDS

With sloping lawns to the south and two formal gardens up near the house, the South Grounds, where the annual Easter Egg Roll is held, are essentially the president's backyard. Historic trees planted here include the Jackson magnolias; a Japanese maple planted by First Lady Frances Cleveland and another by First Lady Rosalynn Carter; four saucer magnolias planted by President John F. Kennedy; and a cedar of Lebanon planted by President Jimmy Carter.

FURTHER READING

Since 1962, the White House Historical Association has maintained a broad-ranging publishing program.
The following publications offer more reading on the history of the President's House,
the White House, the annual Easter Egg Roll, and the White House Grounds:

Garden for the President: A History of the White House Grounds, by Jonathan Pliska. 2016.

The White House Garden, by William Seale. 1996.

The Living White House, by Betty C. Monkman. th edition, 2017.

The White House: An Historic Guide. 24th edition, 2017.

The Presidents of the United States of America. th edition, 2017.

The First Ladies of the United States of America, by Allida Black. 13th edition, 2017.

The White House: The History of an American Idea, by William Seale. 3rd edition, 2018.

The White House: Its Historic Furnishings and First Families, by Betty C. Monkman. 2nd edition, 2014.

White House History Quarterly. The journal of the White House Historical Association published from 1983 to the present: WhiteHouseHistoryJournal.org

For more information visit: WhiteHouseHistory.org

Author **Jonathan W. Pliska** is a landscape historian and author of *A Garden for the President: A History of the White House Grounds*. He has extensively explored and studied documents of the historic White House. He has written and edited Cultural Landscapes Inventories for the National Park Service, including one for the Ellipse, south of the White House Grounds. Jonathan Pliska lives, writes, and plants a garden of his own in Baltimore County, Maryland.

Illustrator **John Hutton** was educated at Princeton, Harvard and the Courtauld Institute of A University of London. He is the author and illustrator of *The Whi House ABC: A Presidential Alphab* and the *Sister Maus* book series Currently professor of art history Salem College, where he has taug since 1990, he resides in Winsto Salem, North Carolina with his wife and three children.